Christmas Songs

By Jennifer M Edwards

Table of Contents

A Child This Day is Born

Author Unknown
Traditional Christmas song

A child this day is born,
A child of high renown,
Most worthy of a sceptre,
A sceptre and a crown.

Glad tidings to all men,
Glad tidings sing we may,
Because the King of kings,
Was born on Christmas day.

These tidings shepherds heard,
Whilst watching over their fold;
'Twas by an Angel unto them,
That night revealed and told.

Glad tidings to all men,
Glad tidings sing we may,
Because the King of kings,
Was born on Christmas day.

To whom the Angel spoke,
Saying, "Be not afraid,
Be glad, poor silly shepherds.
Why are you so dismayed?"

Glad tidings to all men,
Glad tidings sing we may,
Because the King of kings,
Was born on Christmas day.

"For lo! I bring you tidings,
Of gladness and of mirth.
Which cometh to all people by,
This holy infant's birth."

Glad tidings to all men,
Glad tidings sing we may,

Because the King of kings,
Was born on Christmas day.

Then was there with the Angel,
A host incontinent,
Of heavenly bright soldiers,
All from the highest sent.

Glad tidings to all men,
Glad tidings sing we may,
Because the King of kings,
Was born on Christmas day.

They praised the Lord our God,
And our celestial King;
All glory be in Paradise,
This heavenly host do sing.

Glad tidings to all men,
Glad tidings sing we may,
Because the King of kings,
Was born on Christmas day.

And as the Angel told them,
So to them did appear.
They found the young child Jesus Christ,
With Mary, His mother dear.

Glad tidings to all men,
Glad tidings sing we may,
Because the King of kings,
Was born on Christmas day.

All glory be to God,
That sitteth still on high,
With praises and with triumph great,
And joyful melody.

Glad tidings to all men,
Glad tidings sing we may,
Because the King of kings,
Was born on Christmas day.

A Christmas to Remember

Written and Composed by
Amy Grant, Chris Eaton, Beverly Darnall in 1999
Performed by Amy Grant

Twinkling lights
A chill is in the air
And carols everywhere
Close your eyes, it's almost here
Candles and cards
And favourite movie scenes
The smell of evergreen
As special as it's always been
And I have a dream or two
Maybe they will come true

Setting our hopes on a big snow tonight
We'll wake up to a world of white
It's gonna be a Christmas to remember
Light up the fire, play some Nat King Cole
Always sentimental and don't you know that
It's gonna be a Christmas to remember

I know it's true
Time doesn't stand still
Many things can change
But we know some things never will
The memories we share
The songs we always sing
The mystery of life
The hopefulness this season brings
And I have a dream or two
Maybe they will come true

Setting our hopes on a big snow tonight
We'll wake up to a world of white
It's gonna be a Christmas to remember
Light up the fire, play some Nat King Cole
Always sentimental and don't you know that
It's gonna be a Christmas to remember

All I Want for Christmas is You

Written by Mariah Carey and Walter Afanasieff in 1994
Performed by Mariah Carey

I don't want a lot for Christmas,
There is just one thing I need.
I don't care about the presents
Underneath the Christmas tree.
I just want you for my own,
More than you could ever know.
Make my wish come true,
All I want for Christmas is...
You!

I don't want a lot for Christmas,
There is just one thing I need.
I don't care about the presents
Underneath the Christmas tree.
I don't need to hang my stocking,
There upon the fireplace.
Santa Claus won't make me happy,
With a toy on Christmas day.
I just want you for my own,
More than you could ever know.
Make my wish come true,
All I want for Christmas is you...
You baby!

I won't ask for much this Christmas,
I won't even wish for snow.
I'm just gonna keep on waiting,
Underneath the mistletoe.
I won't make a list and send it,
To the North Pole for Saint Nick.
I won't even stay awake to
Hear those magic reindeers click,
'Cause I just want you here tonight,
Holding on to me so tight.
What more can I do,
Baby, all I want for Christmas is you!
You baby!

All the lights are shining,
So brightly everywhere.
And the sound of children's
Laughter fills the air.
And everyone is singing,
I hear those sleigh bells ringing.
Santa won't you bring me the one I really need,
Won't you please bring my baby to me...

Oh, I don't want a lot for Christmas,
This is all I'm asking for.
I just want to see my baby,
Standing right outside my door.
Oh I just want you for my own,
More than you could ever know.
Make my wish come true,
Baby, all I want for Christmas is...
You! You baby!

All I want for Christmas is you...baby!
(repeat and fade)

Angels, From the Realms of Glory

Written by James Montgomery in 1816
Music by Henry T. Smart in 1867

Angels, from the realms of glory,
Wing your flight o'er all the earth;
Ye, who sang creation's story,
Now proclaim Messiah's birth.

Come and worship,
Come and worship,
Worship Christ, the new-born King.

Shepherds in the field abiding,
Watching o'er your flocks by night.
God with man is now residing,
Yonder shines the infant Light.

Come and worship,
Come and worship,
Worship Christ, the new-born King.

Sages, leave your contemplations,
Brighter visions beam afar.
Seek the great Desire of nations,
Ye have seen his natal star.

Come and worship,
Come and worship,
Worship Christ, the new-born King.

Saints before the altar bending,
Watching long in hope and fear,
Suddenly the Lord, descending,
In his temple shall appear.

Come and worship,
Come and worship,
Worship Christ, the new-born King.

Angels Singing, Church Bells Ringing

Author Unknown; German Music

All
Angels singing, church bells ringing,
Holly twining, stars out shining,
Bright with smiles each childish face;
Haste to meet Him, gladly greet Him,
Fall before Him, there adore Him,
Born of Mary, full of Grace.

Choir.
Tell us who is born today
Answer quickly, children, say?

Children
Jesus Christ, our God is born
As a Babe, this Christmas morn.

Choir
Say who brought the tidings down,
Who has made the wonder known?

Children
Thousand angels in the sky
Sang the glorious mystery.

Choir
Say what waters there were found
First to hear the welcome sound?

Children
Shepherds in the fields tonight,
Heard the song and saw the Light

Choir
Rested they beside the fold
When the joyful news was told?

Children
Nay, with loving haste they sped
Unto Bethlehem's cattle-shed.

7

Choir
Quickly say what saw they there,
Did they find the Babe so fair?

Children
Yes, all sweetly on the hay,
Jesus in the manger lay.

Choir
Was He there alone? Were none
Set to guard the Blessed One?

Children
Mary rocked Him on her breast,
Joseph watched the Babe at rest.

Choir
May we too the Babe adore,
Kneeling on the stable-floor?

Children
Yes, we may adore Him thus,
For the Babe is born for us.

Choir
Unto us a Son is given,
God hath made us heirs of Heav'n!
Holy Spirit, Thee we pray,
Draw us hither day by day.

Children
Jesus! To Thy manger bed
May Thy children all be led;
There the Infant Saviour see,
Love and praise and worship Thee.

All
Angels singing, church bells ringing,
Holly twining, stars out shining,
Bright with smiles each childish face;
Haste to meet Him, gladly greet Him,
Fall before Him, there adore Him,
Born of Mary, full of Grace.

Angels We Have Heard on High

Traditional French Carol, "Les Anges dans nos Campagnes"
Translated to English by Bishop James Chadwick in the 1860s

Angels we have heard on high
Sweetly singing o'er the plains
And the mountains in reply
Echoing their joyous strains

Gloria, in Excelsis Deo
Gloria, in Excelsis Deo

Shepherds, why this jubilee?
Why your joyous strains prolong?
What the gladsome tidings be,
Which inspire your heavenly song?

Gloria, in Excelsis Deo
Gloria, in Excelsis Deo

Come to Bethlehem and see
Him whose birth the angels sing;
Come, adore on bended knee,
Christ the Lord, the new-born King.

Gloria, in Excelsis Deo
Gloria, in Excelsis Deo

See Him in a manger laid,
Whom the choirs of angels praise;
Mary, Joseph, lend your aid,
While our hearts in love raise.

Gloria, in Excelsis Deo
Gloria, in Excelsis Deo

As with Gladness, Men of Old

Written by William Chatterton in 1860

As with gladness, men of old
Did the guiding star behold
As with joy they hailed its light
Leading onward, beaming bright
So, most glorious Lord, may we
Evermore be led to Thee

As with joyful steps they sped
To that lowly manger bed
There to bend the knee before
Him whom heaven and earth adore
So may we with willing feet
Ever seek Thy mercy seat

As they offered gifts most rare
At that manger rude and bare
So may we, with holy joy
Pure and free from sin's alloy
All our costliest treasures bring
Christ, to Thee, our heavenly King

Holy Jesus, every day
Keep us in the narrow way
And, when earthly things are past
Bring our ransomed souls at last
Where they need no star to guide
Where no clouds Thy Glory hide

In the heavenly country bright
Need they no created light
Thou its Light, its Joy, its Crown
Thou its Sun which goes not down
There forever may we sing
Hallelujahs to our King

Away in A Manger

Author Unknown
Music composed by James R. Murray

Away in a manger,
No crib for a bed,
The little Lord Jesus,
Laid down His sweet head.

The stars in the bright sky,
Looked down where He lay.
The little Lord Jesus,
Asleep in the hay.

The cattle are lowing,
The baby awakes.
But little Lord Jesus,
No crying He makes.

I love Thee, Lord Jesus,
Look down from the sky,
And stay by my side,
'Til morning is nigh.

Be near me, Lord Jesus,
I ask Thee to stay.
Close by me forever,
And love me, I pray.

Bless all the dear children,
In Thy tender care.
And take us to Heaven,
To live with Thee there.

Baby It's Cold Outside

Duet Written and Composed by Frank Loesser in 1944
Frank Loesser premiered the song with his wife at their Navarro Hotel
housewarming party.
Recorded by Johnny Mercer and Margaret Whiting in 1949

Female lyrics
(Male lyrics)

I really can't stay
(But, baby, it's cold outside)

I've got to go 'way
(But, baby, it's cold outside)

This evening has been
(Been hoping that you'd drop in)

So very nice
(I'll hold your hands, they're just like ice)

My mother will start to worry
(Beautiful, what's your hurry)

My father will be pacing the floor
(Listen to the fireplace roar)

So really I'd better scurry
(Beautiful, please don't hurry)

Well maybe just a half a drink more
(Put some records on while I pour)

The neighbours might think
(Baby, it's bad out there)

Say, what's in this drink?
(No cabs to be had out there)

I wish I knew how
(Your eyes are like starlight now)

To break this spell
(I'll take your hat, your hair looks swell)

I ought to say no, no, no, sir
(Mind if I move in closer?)

At least I'm gonna say that I tried
(What's the sense in hurting my pride?)

I really can't stay
(Oh, baby, don't hold out)

Ahh, but it's cold outside
(Baby, it's cold outside)

I simply must go
(But, baby, it's cold outside)

The answer is no
(But, baby, it's cold outside)

This welcome has been
(How lucky that you dropped in)

So nice and warm
(Look out the window at that storm)

My sister will be suspicious
(Gosh, your lips look delicious)

My brother will be there at the door
(Waves upon a tropical shore)

My maiden aunt's mind is vicious
(Ohh, your lips are delicious)

Well maybe just a cigarette more
(Never such a blizzard before)

I've got to get home
(But, baby, you'll freeze out there)

Say, lend me your coat
(It's up to your knees out there)

You've really been grand
(I'm thrilled when you touch my hand)

But don't you see
(How can you do this thing to me?)

There's bound to be talk tomorrow
(Think of my lifelong sorrow)

At least there will be plenty implied
(If you caught pneumonia and died)

I really can't stay
(Get over that old doubt)

Aw, but it's cold outside
(Oooo, baby it's cold outside)

Blue Christmas

Written by Bill Hayes and Jay Johnson
Performed by Doye O'Dell in 1948
Elvis Presley and many others have also performed this song

I'll have a blue Christmas without you,
I'll be so blue thinking about you.
Decorations of red,
On a green Christmas tree.
Won't be the same, dear,
If you're not here with me.

And when those blue snowflakes start fallin',
And when those blue memories start callin';
You'll be doing all right with your Christmas of white,
But I'll have a blue, blue, blue, blue Christmas.

I'll have a blue Christmas, that's certain,
And when that blue heartache starts hurting.
You'll be doing all right,
With your Christmas of white,
But I'll have a blue, blue Christmas.

Carol of the Bells

Composed by Mykola Dmytrovich Leontovych
Based on a Ukrainian carol
Translated to English by Peter J. Wilhousky.

Hark how the bells,
Sweet silver bells,
All seem to say,
Throw cares away.

Christmas is here,
Bringing good cheer,
To young and old,
Meek and the bold.

Ding dong, ding dong,
That is their song,
With joyful ring,
All caroling.

One seems to hear,
Words of good cheer,
From everywhere,
Filling the air.

Oh, how they pound,
Raising the sound,
O'er hill and dale,
Telling their tale.

Gaily they ring,
While people sing
Songs of good cheer,
Christmas is here.

Merry, Merry, Merry, Merry Christmas,
Merry, Merry, Merry, Merry Christmas.
On on they send,
On without end,
Their joyful tone,
To every home.
Ding dong, ding...dong!

Caroling, Caroling

Alfred Burt and Wilha Hutson in 1954

Caroling, caroling, now we go
Christmas bells are ringing
Caroling, caroling through the snow
Christmas bells are ringing

Joyous voices sweet and clear
Sing the sad of heart to cheer
Ding dong, ding dong
Christmas bells are ringing

Caroling, caroling through the town
Christmas bells are ringing
Caroling, caroling up and down
Christmas bells are ringing

Mark ye well the song we sing
Gladsome tidings now we bring
Ding dong, ding dong
Christmas bells are ringing!

Caroling, caroling, near and far
Christmas bells are ringing
Following, following yonder star
Christmas bells are ringing

Sing we all this happy morn
"Lo, the King of heav'n is born!"
Ding dong, ding dong
Christmas bells are ringing

Christ is Born in Bethlehem

This song is extracted from "Hark, the Herald Angels Sing"
Written by Charles Wesley and Music by Felix Mendelssohn

Christ, by highest heaven adored
Christ, the everlasting Lord;
Late in time behold Him come
Offspring of a virgin's womb.
Veiled in flesh the Godhead see;
Hail the Incarnate Deity,
Pleased as man with man to dwell;
Jesus, our Emmanuel.

Come, desire of nations come,
Fix in us Thy humble home;
Rise, the Woman's conquering Seed,
Bruise in us the Serpent's head.
Adam's likeness, Lord efface:
Stamp Thy image in its place;
Second Adam, from above,
Reinstate us in Thy love.

Hail, the Heaven-born Prince of Peace!
Hail, the Son of Righteousness!
Light and life to all He brings,
Ris'n with haling in His wings.
Mild He lays His glory by,
Born that man no more may die,
Born to raise the sons of earth.

C-H-R-I-S-T-M-A-S

Written by Jenny Lou Carson
Composed by Eddy Arnold in 1961

When I was but a youngster,
Christmas meant one thing,
That I'd be getting lots of toys that day.
I learned a whole lot different,
When my Mother sat me down,
And taught me to spell Christmas this way:

"C" is for the Christ child, born upon this day,
"H" for herald angels in the night,
"R" means our Redeemer,
"I" means Israel,
"S" is for the star that shone so bright,
"T" is for three wise men, they who traveled far,
"M" is for the manger where He lay,
"A" is for all He stands for,
"S" means shepherds came,

And that's why there's a Christmas day,
And that's why there's a Christmas day.

Christmas is A-Comin' (May God Bless You)

Written by Frank Luther and Composed by John Purifoy
Performed by Bing Crosby in 1953

When I'm feeling blue and when I'm feeling low,
Then I start to think about the happiest man I know.
He doesn't mind the snow and he doesn't mind the rain,
But all December you will hear him at your window pane,
A-singing again and again and again and again and again and again.

Christmas is a-comin' and the bells begin to ring,
The holly's in the window and the birds begin to sing.
Now I don't take time to worry and I don't take time to fret,
And the more you give at Christmas time the more you'll get.

God bless you, gentlemen, God bless you!
And the more you give at Christmas time the more you get.

Christmas is a-comin' and the egg is in the nog.
Pleased to give a friendly man a friendly little dog.
If you haven't got a friendly dog, a friendly cat will do,
If you haven't got a friendly cat, may God bless you!

God bless you, gentlemen, God bless you!
If you haven't got a friendly cat, may God bless you!

Christmas is a-comin' and the lights are on the tree.
How about a turkey leg for poor old me?
If you haven't got a turkey leg, a turkey wing will do.
If you haven't got a turkey wing, may God bless you!

God bless you, gentlemen, God bless you!
If you haven't got a turkey wing, may God bless you!

Christmas is a-comin' and the ciders in the keg.
If I had a mug of cider then I wouldn't have to beg.
If you haven't got a mug of cider, half a mug will do.
If you haven't got a half a mug, may God bless you!

God bless you, gentlemen, God bless you!
If you haven't got half a mug, may God bless you!
If you haven't got a thing for me, may God bless you!

Christmas Time is Here

From "A Charlie Brown Christmas"
Performed by Vince Guaraldi Trio in 1965

Christmas time is here
Happiness and cheer
Fun for all that children call
Their favourite time of year

Snowflakes in the air
Carols everywhere
Olden times and ancient rhymes
Of love and dreams to share

Sleigh bells in the air
Beauty everywhere
Yuletide by the fireside
And joyful memories there

Christmas time is here
Families drawing near
Oh, that we could always see
Such spirit through the year

Oh, that we could always see
Such spirit through the year...

Deck the Halls

Author Unknown
Traditional Welsh Carol
Translated to English by J.P. McCaskey in 1881

Deck the halls with boughs of holly,
Fa la la la la, la la la la.
'Tis the season to be jolly,
Fa la la la la, la la la la.

Don we now our gay apparel,
Fa la la la la, la la la la.
Troll the ancient Yuletide carol,
Fa la la la la, la la la la.

See the blazing Yule before us,
Fa la la la la, la la la la.
Strike the harp and join the chorus,
Fa la la la la, la la la la.

Follow me in merry measure,
Fa la la la la, la la la la.
While I tell of Yuletide treasure,
Fa la la la la, la la la la.

Fast away the old year passes,
Fa la la la la, la la la la.
Hail the new, ye lads and lasses,
Fa la la la la, la la la la.

Sing we joyous, all together,
Fa la la la la, la la la la.
Heedless of the wind and weather,
Fa la la la la, la la la la.

Ding Dong! Merrily on High!

Written by George Ratcliffe Woodward in 1924
Composed by Charles Wood

Ding Dong! Merrily on high,
In heav'n the bells are ringing;
Ding, dong! Verily the sky,
Is riv'n with angel singing,
Gloria, Hosanna in Excelsis!

E'en so here below, below,
Let steeple bells be swungen,
And "I-o, i-o, i-o!"
By priest and people be sungen.
Gloria, Hosanna in Excelsis!

Pray ye dutifully prime,
Your matin chime, ye ringers;
May ye beautifully rime,
Your evetime song, ye singers.
Gloria, Hosanna in Excelsis!

Do They Know It's Christmas?

Written by Bob Geldof
Composed by Midge Ure
Performed by Band Aid
Released in 1984
To raise money for relief of the 1983-1985 famine in Ethiopia

It's Christmas time
There's no need to be afraid
At Christmas time
We let in light and we banish shade

And in our world of plenty
We can spread a smile of joy
Throw your arms around the world
At Christmas time

But say a prayer to
Pray for the other ones
At Christmas time

It's hard, but when you're having fun
There's a world outside your window
And it's a world of dreaded fear
Where the only water flowing
Is the bitter sting of tears

And the Christmas bells that ring there
Are the clanging chimes of doom
Well, tonight, thank God, it's them
Instead of you

And there won't be snow in Africa
This Christmas time
The greatest gift they'll get this year is life
Where nothing ever grows
No rain or rivers flow

Do they know it's Christmas time at all?

Here's to you
Raise a glass for everyone

Here's to them
Underneath that burning sun

Do they know it's Christmas time at all?

Feed the world
Feed the world
Feed the world
Let them know it's Christmas time and
Feed the world
Let them know it's Christmas time and
Feed the world
Let them know it's Christmas time and
Feed the world
Let them know it's Christmas time and
Feed the world
Let them know it's Christmas time and
Feed the world
Let them know it's Christmas time

Do You Hear What I Hear?

Written by Noel Regney and Gloria Shayne in 1962

Said the night wind to the little lamb,
Do you see what I see?
Way up in the sky, little lamb,
Do you see what I see?
A star, a star, dancing in the night,
With a tail as big as a kite,
With a tail as big as a kite.

Said the little lamb to the shepherd boy,
Do you hear what I hear?
Ringing through the sky, shepherd boy,
Do you hear what I hear?
A song, a song, high above the trees,
With a voice as big as the sea,
With a voice as big as the sea.

Said the shepherd boy to the mighty King,
Do you know what I know?
In your palace warm, mighty King,
Do you know what I know?
A child, a child shivers in the cold,
Let us bring Him silver and gold,
Let us bring Him silver and gold.

Said the king to the people everywhere,
Listen to what I say.
Pray for peace, people everywhere,
Listen to what I say.
The child, the child, sleeping in the night,
He will bring us goodness and light,
He will bring us goodness and light.

Feliz Navidad

Written and performed by José Feliciano in 1970

Feliz Navidad
Feliz Navidad
Feliz Navidad
Prospero Año y Felicidad

Feliz Navidad
Feliz Navidad
Feliz Navidad
Prospero Año y Felicidad

I wanna wish you a Merry Christmas
I wanna wish you a Merry Christmas
I wanna wish you a Merry Christmas
From the bottom of my heart

[repeat all]

Actual Translation:

Merry Christmas
Merry Christmas
Merry Christmas
Prosperous New Year and Happiness

Frosty the Snowman

Written by Steve "Jack" Rollins and Steve Nelson in 1950
The television special was made based on this song

Frosty the Snowman
Was a jolly happy soul,
With a corncob pipe and a button nose,
And two eyes made out of coal.

Frosty the Snowman
Is a fairy tale, they say,
He was made of snow,
But the children know
How he came to life one day.

There must have been some magic
In that old silk hat they found.
For when they placed it on his head,
He began to dance around.

Frosty the Snowman
Was alive as he could be,
And the children say he could laugh
And play just the same as you and me.

Thumpety thump thump,
Thumpety thump thump,
Look at Frosty go!
Thumpety thump thump,
Thumpety thump thump,
Over the hills of snow!

Frosty the Snowman
Knew the sun was hot that day,
So he said, "Let's run
And we'll have some fun
Now before I melt away."

Down to the village,
With a broomstick in his hand,
Running here and there,

All around the square saying,
"Catch me if you can."

He led them down the streets of town,
Right to the traffic cop.
And he only paused a moment when
He heard him holler "Stop!"

Frosty the Snowman
Had to hurry on his way,
But he waved goodbye saying,
"Don't you cry,
I'll be back again someday."

Thumpety thump thump,
Thumpety thump thump,
Look at Frosty go!
Thumpety thump thump,
Thumpety thump thump,
Over the hills of snow!

Go, Tell It on the Mountain

Written by John Wesley Work, Jr. in 1907

While shepherds kept their watching
O'er silent flocks by night,
Behold throughout the heavens
There shone a holy light

Go, tell it on the mountain
Over the hills and everywhere
Go, tell it on the mountain
That Jesus Christ is born

The shepherds feared and trembled
When lo! Above the earth
Rang out the angel chorus
That hailed our Saviour's birth

Go, tell it on the mountain
Over the hills and everywhere
Go, tell it on the mountain
That Jesus Christ is born

Down in a lowly manger
The humble Christ was born
And God sent out salvation
That blessed Christmas morn

God Rest Ye Merry, Gentlemen

Traditional English Carol
First published in 1833

God rest ye merry, gentlemen,
Let nothing you dismay.
Remember, Christ, our Saviour,
Was born on Christmas day;
To save us all from Satan's power,
When we were gone astray.

O tidings of comfort and joy,
Comfort and joy,
O tidings of comfort and joy.

In Bethlehem, in Israel,
This blessed Babe was born,
And laid within a manger,
Upon this blessed morn;
The which His Mother Mary,
Did nothing take in scorn.

O tidings of comfort and joy,
Comfort and joy,
O tidings of comfort and joy.

From God our heavenly Father,
A blessed angel came.
And unto certain shepherds,
Brought tidings of the same.
How that in Bethlehem was born,
The Son of God by name.

O tidings of comfort and joy,
Comfort and joy,
O tidings of comfort and joy.

"Fear not then," said the angel,
"Let nothing you affright,
This day is born a Saviour,
Of a pure virgin bright.

To free all those who trust in Him,
From Satan's power and might."

O tidings of comfort and joy,
Comfort and joy,
O tidings of comfort and joy.

The shepherds at those tidings,
Rejoiced much in mind,
And left their flocks a-feeding,
In tempest, storm and wind;
And went to Bethlehem straightway,
The Son of God to find.

O tidings of comfort and joy,
Comfort and joy,
O tidings of comfort and joy.

And when they came to Bethlehem,
Where our dear Saviour lay,
They found Him in a manger,
Where oxen feed on hay;
His Mother Mary kneeling down,
Unto the Lord did pray.

O tidings of comfort and joy,
Comfort and joy,
O tidings of comfort and joy.

Now to the Lord sing praises,
All you within this place,
And with true love and brotherhood,
Each other now embrace;
This holy tide of Christmas,
All other doth deface.

O tidings of comfort and joy,
Comfort and joy,
O tidings of comfort and joy.

Happy Christmas (War is Over)

Written and performed by John Lennon and Yoko Ono in 1971
Along with the Harlem Community Choir

So this is Christmas
And what have you done
Another year over
And a new one just begun

And so this is Christmas
I hope you have fun
The near and the dear ones
The old and the young

A very merry Christmas
And a happy New Year
Let's hope it's a good one
Without any fear

And so this is Christmas
For weak and for strong
The rich and the poor ones
The world is so wrong

And so happy Christmas
For black and for white
For yellow and red ones
Let's stop all the fight

A very merry Christmas
And a happy New Year
Let's hope it's a good one
Without any fear

And so this is Christmas
And what have we done
Another year over
And a new one just begun

And so happy Christmas
We hope you have fun

The near and the dear ones
The old and the young

A very merry Christmas
And a happy New Year
Let's hope it's a good one
Without any fear

War is over
If you want it
War is over
Now...

Happy Holiday
(The Holiday Season)

Written and Composed by Irving Berlin in 1942
Performed by Bing Crosby and Martha Mears in 1942
Performed by Andy Williams in 1953

Happy holiday
Happy holiday
While the merry bells keep ringing
May your every wish come true

Happy holiday
Happy holiday
May the calendar keep bringing
Happy holidays to you

It's the holiday season
And Santa Claus is coming back
The Christmas snow is white on the ground
When old Santa gets into town
He'll be coming down the chimney, down
Coming down the chimney, down

It's the holiday season
And Santa Claus has got a toy
For every good girl and good little boy

He's a great big bundle of joy
He'll be coming down the chimney, down
Coming down the chimney, down

He'll have a big fat pack upon his back
And lots of goodies for you and me
So leave a peppermint stick for old St. Nick
Hanging on the Christmas tree

It's the holiday season
With the whoop-de-do and hickory dock
And don't forget to hang up your sock
'Cause just exactly at 12 o'clock
He'll be coming down the chimney
Coming down the chimney
Coming down the chimney, down

Happy holiday
Happy holiday
While the merry bells keep bringing
Happy holidays to you

Happy holiday
Happy holiday
May the calendar keep bringing
Happy holidays to you
To you
Happy holiday
Happy holiday
Happy holiday...

Hark! The Herald Angels Sing

Written by Charles Wesley
Music by Felix Mendelssohn in 1739

Hark! The herald angels sing,
"Glory to the new-born King!"

Peace on earth and mercy mild
God and sinners reconciled.
Joyful, all ye nations rise,
Join the triumph of the skies;
With the angelic host proclaim:
"Christ is born in Bethlehem"

Hark! The herald angels sing,
"Glory to the new-born King!"

Christ by highest heav'n adored,
Christ the everlasting Lord!
Late in time behold Him come,
Offspring of a virgin's womb.
Veiled in flesh the Godhead see,
Hail the incarnate Deity.
Pleased as man with man to dwell,
Jesus, our Emmanuel.

Hark! The herald angels sing,
"Glory to the new-born King!"

Hail the Heaven-born Prince of Peace!
Hail the Song of Righteousness!
Light and life to all He brings,
Ris'n with healing in His wings.
Mild He lays His glory by,
Born that man no more may die.
Born to raise the sons of earth,
Born to give them second birth.

Hark! The herald angels sing,
"Glory to the new-born King!"

Have Yourself A Merry Little Christmas

Written by Ralph Blane
Music by Hugh Martin
Performed by Judy Garland and other various artists

Have yourself a merry little Christmas.
Let your heart be light.
From now on, our troubles
Will be out of sight.

Have yourself a merry little Christmas.
Make the Yuletide gay.
From now on our troubles
Will be miles away.

Here we are as in olden days,
Happy golden days of yore.
Faithful friends who are dear to us
Gather near to us, once more.

Through the years
We all will be together
If the fates allow.
Hang a shining star
On the highest bough,
And have yourself
A merry little Christmas now.

Here Comes Santa Claus

Written by Gene Autry and Oakley Haldeman in 1947
Performed by Gene Autry

Here comes Santa Claus!
Here comes Santa Claus!
Right down Santa Claus lane!
Vixen and Blitzen and all his reindeer,
Are pulling on the reins.

Bells are ringing, children singing,
All is merry and bright.
Hang your stockings,
And say your prayers,
'Cause Santa Claus comes tonight.

Here comes Santa Claus!
Here comes Santa Claus!
Right down Santa Claus lane!
He's got a bag that is filled with toys,
For the boys and girls again.

Hear those sleigh bells jingle, jingle,
What a beautiful sight.
Jump in bed, cover up your head,
'Cause Santa Claus comes tonight.

Here comes Santa Claus!
Here comes Santa Claus!
Right down Santa Claus lane!
He doesn't care if your rich or poor,
He loves you just the same.

Santa Claus knows that we're all God's children,
That makes everything right.
Fill your hearts with Christmas cheer,
'Cause Santa Claus comes tonight.

Here comes Santa Claus!
Here comes Santa Claus!
Right down Santa Claus lane!

He'll come around when church rings out,
Its Christmas morn again!

Peace on earth will come to all,
If we just follow the light.
Let's give thanks to the Lord above,
'Cause Santa Claus comes tonight.

Holly Jolly Christmas

Written by Johnny Marks
Recorded by Burl Ives in 1965

Have a holly, jolly Christmas,
It's the best time of the year.
I don't know if there'll be snow,
But have a cup of cheer.

Have a holly, jolly Christmas,
And when you walk down the street.
Say hello to friends you know,
And everyone you meet.

Oh ho, the mistletoe,
Hung where you can see.
Somebody waits for you,
Kiss her once for me.

Have a holly, jolly Christmas,
And in case you didn't hear,
Oh by golly,
Have a holly, jolly Christmas,
This year!

(There's No Place Like)
Home for the Holidays

Written by Al Stillman and Composed by Robert Allen
Performed by Perry Como in 1954 and by The Carpenters in 1984

Oh! There's no place like home for the holidays,
'Cause no matter how far away you roam,
When you pine for the sunshine of a friendly gaze,
For the holidays you can't beat home sweet home!

I met a man who lives in Tennessee, he was headin' for,
Pennsylvania and some homemade pumpkin pie!
From Pennsylvania folks are travelin',
Down the Dixie sunny shore,
From Atlantic to Pacific,
Gee the traffic is terrific!

Oh! There's no place like home for the holidays,
'Cause no matter how far away you roam,
If you want to be happy in a million ways,
For the holidays you can't beat home sweet home!

Take a bus, take a train, go and hop an aeroplane,
Put the wife an' kiddies in the family car!
For the pleasure that you bring when you make that doorbell ring,
No trip could be too far!

I met a man who lives in Tennessee, he was headin' for,
Pennsylvania and some homemade pumpkin pie!
(Some pumpkin pie!)
From Pennsylvania folks are travelin',
Down the Dixie sunny shore,
From Atlantic to Pacific,
Gee the traffic is terrific!

Oh! There's no place like home for the holidays,
'Cause no matter how far away you roam,
If you want to be happy in a million ways,
For the holidays you can't beat home sweet home!
For the holidays you can't beat home sweet home!

I Heard the Bells on Christmas Day

Written by Henry Wadsworth Longfellow in 1863
Composed by John Baptist Calkin in 1872
Performed by various artists including Elvis Presley
Also composed by Johnny Marks in the 1950s
This version also performed by various artists including Frank Sinatra

I heard the bells on Christmas day
Their old familiar carols play
And mild and sweet the words repeat,
Of peace on earth, good will to men.

I thought how as the day had come,
The belfries of all Christendom
Had rolled along the unbroken song
Of peace on earth, good will to men.

And in despair I bowed my head,
"There is no peace on earth," I said,
"For hate is strong, and mocks the song
Of peace on earth, good will to men."

Then pealed the bells more loud and deep,
"God is not dead, nor doth He sleep;
The wrong shall fail, the right prevail,
With peace on earth, good will to men."

'Til ringing, singing on its way,
The world revolved from night to day,
A voice, a chime, a chant sublime,
Of peace on earth, good will to men!

I Saw Mommy Kissing Santa Claus

Written by Tommie Connor in 1952

I saw Mommy kissing Santa Claus
Underneath the mistletoe last night.
She didn't see me creep
Down the stairs to have a peek.
She thought that I was tucked
Up in my bedroom fast asleep.

Then, I saw Mommy tickle Santa Claus
Underneath his beard so snowy white.
Oh what a laugh it would have been,
If Daddy had only seen
Mommy kissing Santa Claus last night.

I'll Be Home for Christmas

Written and Composed by Kim Gannon, Walter Kent, and Buck Ram
Performed by Bing Crosby in 1943

I'm dreaming tonight
Of a place I love
Even more than I usually do
And although I know
It's a long road back
I promise you

I'll be home for Christmas
You can count on me
Please have snow and mistletoe
And presents on the tree

Christmas Eve will find me
Where the love light gleams
I'll be home for Christmas
If only in my dreams

I'll be home for Christmas
You can count on me
Please have snow and mistletoe
And presents on the tree

Christmas Eve will find me
Where the love light gleams
I'll be home for Christmas
If only in my dreams

It Must Have Been the Mistletoe

Written by Justin Wilde and Doug Konecky in 1979
Performed by Barbara Mandrell in 1984
Performed by other various artists since

It must have been the mistletoe
The lazy fire, the falling snow
The magic in the frosty air
That feeling everywhere

It must have been the pretty lights
That glistened in the silent night
Or maybe just the stars so bright
That shined above you

Our first Christmas
More than we'd been dreaming of
Old Saint Nicholas had his fingers crossed
That we would fall in love!

It could have been the holiday
The midnight ride upon a sleigh
The countryside all dressed in white
That crazy snowball fight!

It could have been the steeple bell
That wrapped us up in its spell
It only took one kiss to know
It must have been the mistletoe!

Our first Christmas
More than we'd been dreaming of
Old Saint Nicholas must have known that kiss
Would lead to all of this!!

It must have been the mistletoe
The lazy fire, the falling snow
The magic in the frosty air
That made me love you!

On Christmas Eve a wish came true
The night I fell in love with you

43

It only took one kiss to know
It must have been the mistletoe!

It must have been the mistletoe
The lazy fire, the falling snow
The magic in the frosty air
That feeling everywhere

It must have been the mistletoe
The lazy fire, the falling snow
The magic in the frosty air
That made me love you

It must have been the mistletoe
The lazy fire, the falling snow
The magic in the frosty air
That feeling everywhere

It's Beginning to Look A Lot Like Christmas

Written and Composed by Meredith Wilson in 1951
Performed by Perry Como and the Fontane Sisters with Mitchell Ayres &
his orchestra in 1951
Also Performed by Bing Crosby in 1951

It's beginning to look a lot like Christmas
Everywhere you go
Take a look in the five-and-ten
Glistening once again
With candy canes and silver lanes aglow

It's beginning to look a lot like Christmas
Toys in every store
But the prettiest sight to see
Is the holly that will be
On your own front door

A pair of hop-along boots
And a pistol that shoots
Is the wish of Barney and Ben
Dolls that will talk
And will go for a walk
Is the hope of Janice and Jen
And Mom and Dad can hardly wait
For school to start again

It's beginning to look a lot like Christmas
Everywhere you go
There's a tree in the Grand Hotel
One in the park as well
The sturdy kind that doesn't mind the snow

It's beginning to look a lot like Christmas
Soon the bells will start
And the thing that will make them ring
Is the carol that you sing
Right within your heart

It's the Most Wonderful Time of the Year

Written and Composed by Edward Pola and George Wyle in 1963
Performed by Andy Williams

It's the most wonderful time of the year
With the kids jingle belling
And everyone telling you "Be of good cheer"
It's the most wonderful time of the year

It's the hap-happiest season of all
With those holiday greetings
And gay happy meetings
When friends come to call
It's the hap-happiest season of all

There'll be parties for hosting
Marshmallows for toasting
And caroling out in the snow
There'll be scary ghost stories and
Tales of the glories of Christmases long, long ago

It's the most wonderful time of the year
There'll be much mistletoe-ing
And hearts will be glowing
When loved ones are near
It's the most wonderful time of the year

There'll be parties for hosting
Marshmallows for toasting
And caroling out in the snow
There'll be scary ghost stories and
Tales of the glories of Christmases long, long ago

It's the most wonderful time of the year
There'll be much mistletoe-ing
And hearts will be glowing
When loved ones are near

It's the most wonderful time
It's the most wonderful time
It's the most wonderful time of the year

Jesus, Born on This Day

Written by Mariah Carey and Walter Afanasieff in 1994

Today a child is born on earth,
Today a child is born on earth.
Today the glory of God,
Shines everywhere, for all of the world.

Oh Jesus born on this day,
He is our light and salvation.
Oh Jesus born on this day,
He is the King of all nations.

Behold the Lamb of God has come,
Behold the Lamb of God has come.
Behold the Saviour is born,
Sing of His love, to everyone.

Oh Jesus born on this day,
Heavenly Child in a manger.
Oh Jesus born on this day,
He is our Lord and our Saviour.

Today our hearts rejoice in him,
Today our hearts rejoice in him.
Today the light of His birth,
Fills us with hope, and brings peace on earth.

Oh Jesus born on this day,
He is our light and salvation.
Oh Jesus born on this day,
He is the King of all nations.
Today a child is born on earth,
Today a child is born on earth.

He is light, He is love, He is grace,
Born on Christmas day.
He is light, He is love, He is grace,
Born on Christmas day.
He is light, He is love, He is grace,
Born on Christmas day.

Jingle Bell Rock

Written by Hank Garland
Composed by Joseph Carleton Beal and James Ross Boothe
Performed by Bobby Helms in 1957

Jingle bell, jingle bell, jingle bell rock,
Jingle bells swing and jingle bells ring.
Snowing and blowing up bushels of fun,
Now the jingle hop has begun.

Jingle bell, jingle bell, jingle bell rock,
Jingle bells chime in jingle bell time.
Dancing and prancing in Jingle Bell Square,
In the frosty air.

What a bright time, it's the right time,
To rock the night away.
Jingle bell time is a swell time,
To go gliding in a one-horse sleigh.

Giddy-up jingle horse,
Pick up your feet,
Jingle around the clock,
Mix and a-mingle in the jingling feet.

That's the jingle bell,
That's the jingle bell,
That's the jingle bell rock!

Jingle Bells

Written and Composed by James Lord Pierpont in 1857
Original Title was "One Horse Open Sleigh"
Often thought to be a Christmas song, it was actually written and
sung for Thanksgiving

Dashing through the snow
In a one horse open sleigh,
Over the fields we go,
Laughing all the way;
Bells on bob-tails ring,
Making spirits bright,
What fun it is to laugh and sing
A sleighing song tonight.

Jingle bells, jingle bells,
Jingle all the way!
Oh, what fun it is to ride,
In a one horse open sleigh!
(Optional repeat)

A day or two ago,
I thought I'd take a ride,
And soon Miss Fanny Bright
Was seated by my side;
The horse was lean and lank;
Misfortune seemed his lot;
He got into a drifted bank,
And then, we got up sot.

Jingle bells, jingle bells,
Jingle all the way!
Oh, what fun it is to ride,
In a one horse open sleigh!
(Optional repeat)

A day or two ago,
The story I must tell,
I went out on the snow,
And on my back I fell;
A gent was riding by,
In a one horse open sleigh,

He laughed as there I sprawling lie,
But quickly drove away.

Jingle bells, jingle bells,
Jingle all the way!
Oh, what fun it is to ride,
In a one horse open sleigh!
(Optional repeat)

Now the ground is white,
Go it while you're young,
Take the girls tonight,
And sing this sleighing song;
Just get a bob-tailed bay,
Two-forty as his speed,
Hitch him to an open sleigh,
And crack! You'll take the lead.

Jingle bells, jingle bells,
Jingle all the way!
Oh, what fun it is to ride,
In a one horse open sleigh!
(Optional repeat)

Jolly Old Saint Nicholas

Author Unknown
Composed by Tom Hall

Jolly old Saint Nicholas,
Lean your ear this way!
Don't you tell a single soul,
What I'm going to say.

Christmas Eve is coming soon,
Now, you dear old man,
Whisper what you'll bring to me,
Tell me if you can.

When the clock is striking twelve,
When I'm fast asleep.
Down the chimney broad and black,
With your pack you'll creep.

All the stockings you will find,
Hanging in a row,
Min will be the shortest one,
You'll be sure to know.

Johnny wants a pair of skates,
Susy wants a dolly,
Nellie wants a story book,
She thinks dolls are folly.

As for me, my little brain,
Isn't very bright.
Choose for me, old Santa Claus,
What you think is right.

Joy to the World

Written by Isaac Watts in 1719
Based on the Psalms of David

Joy to the world, the Lord is come!
Let Earth receive her King;
Let every heart prepare Him room,
And heaven and nature sing,
And heaven and nature sing,
And heaven, and heaven, and nature sing.

Joy to the world, the Saviour reigns!
Let men their songs employ;
While fields and floods, rocks, hills and plains
Repeat the sounding joy,
Repeat the sounding joy,
Repeat, repeat, the sounding joy.

No more let sins and sorrows grow,
Nor thorns infest the ground;
He comes to make His blessings flow
Far as the curse is found,
Far as the curse is found,
Far as, far as, the curse is found.

He rules the world with truth and grace,
And makes the nations prove
The glories of His righteousness,
And wonders of His love,
And wonders of His love,
And wonders, wonders, of His love.

Let It Snow! Let It Snow! Let It Snow!

Written by Sammy Cahn in 1945
Composed by Jule Styne in 1945
Performed by Vaughn Monroe in 1945
Performed by Dean Martin in 1959
Performed by other various artists over the years

Oh, the weather outside is frightful,
But the fire is so delightful,
And since we've no place to go,
Let it snow! Let it snow! Let it snow!

It doesn't show signs of stopping,
And I've bought some corn for popping.
The lights are turned way down low,
Let it snow! Let it snow! Let it snow!

When we finally kiss goodnight,
How I'll hate going out in the storm.
But if you'll really hold me tight,
All the way home I'll be warm.

The fire is slowly dying,
And, my dear, we're still goodbye-ing.
But as long as you love me so,
Let it snow! Let it snow! Let it snow!

Little Drummer Boy

Based on a Czech Christmas Carol
Translated to English by Katherine K. Davis
Music by Henry Onorati and Harry Simeone
In 1958

Come they told me
Pa rum pum pum pum
A new-born King to see
Pa rum pum pum pum

Our finest gifts we bring
Pa rum pum pum pum
To lay before the King
Pa rum pum pum pum
Rum pum pum pum
Rum pum pum pum

So to honour Him
Pa rum pum pum pum
When we come

Little baby
Pa rum pum pum pum
I am a poor boy too
Pa rum pum pum pum
I have no gift to bring
Pa rum pum pum pum
That's fit to give our King
Pa rum pum pum pum
Rum pum pum pum
Rum pum pum pum

Shall I play for you
Pa rum pum pum pum
On my drum?

Mary nodded
Pa rum pum pum pum
The ox and lamb kept time
Pa rum pum pum pum
I played my drum for Him

Pa rum pum pum pum
I played my best for Him
Pa rum pum pum pum
Rum pum pum pum
Rum pum pum pum

Then He smiled at me
Pa rum pum pum pum
Me and my drum

Little Saint Nick

Written and Composed by Brian Wilson and Mike Love in 1963
Performed by their group The Beach Boys in 1963

Oooooooo
Merry Christmas Saint Nick
Christmas comes this time each year

Well way up north where the air gets cold
There's a tale about Christmas
That you've all been told
And a real famous cat all dressed up in red
And he spends all year workin' out on his sled

It's the little Saint Nick
Little Saint Nick
It's the little Saint Nick
Little Saint Nick

Just a little bobsled we call it Old Saint Nick
But she'll walk a toboggan with a four speed stick
She's candy apple red with a ski for a wheel
And when Santa hits the gas, man just watch her peel

It's the little Saint Nick
Little Saint Nick
It's the little Saint Nick
Little Saint Nick

Run run reindeer
Run run reindeer
Whoaa
Run run reindeer
Run run reindeer

He don't miss no one

And haulin' through the snow at a frightening speed
With a half a dozen deer with Rudy to lead
He's got to wear his goggles cause the snow really flies
And he's cruisin' every path with a little surprise

It's the little Saint Nick
Little Saint Nick
It's the little Saint Nick
Little Saint Nick

Oooooooo
Merry Christmas Saint Nick
Christmas comes this time each year

Oooooooo
Merry Christmas Saint Nick
Christmas comes this time each year

Oooooooo
Merry Christmas Saint Nick
Christmas comes this time each year

Marshmallow World

Written by Carl Sigman in 1949
Composed by Peter DeRose in 1949
Performed by Bing Crosby in 1950
Performed by Dean Martin and Frank Sinatra in 1967

It's a marshmallow world in the winter
When the snow comes to cover the ground
It's the time for play, it's a whipped cream day
I wait for it the whole year round

Those are marshmallow clouds being friendly
In the arms of the evergreen trees
And the sun is red like a pumpkin head
It's shining so your nose won't freeze

The world is your snowball, see how it grows
That's how it goes, whenever it snows
The world is your snowball, just for a song
Get out and roll it along

It's a yum-yummy world made for sweethearts
Take a walk with your favourite girl
It's a sugar date, what if spring is late
In winter, it's a marshmallow world

It's a marshmallow day in the winter
When the snow comes to cover the ground
It's the time for play, it's a whipped cream day
And we wait for it the whole year round

(Just you remember that)
Those are marshmallow clouds being friendly
In the arms of the evergreen trees
And the sun is red like a pumpkin head
It's shining so your nose won't freeze

(You must remember that)
The world is your snowball, see how it grows
That's how it goes, whenever it snows
The world is your snowball just for a song
Get out and roll it along

It's a yum-yummy world made for sweethearts
Take a walk with your favourite girl
It's a sugar date, what if spring is late
In winter, it's a marshmallow world
In winter, it's a marshmallow world
In winter, it's a marshmallow world

Merry Christmas, Darling

Written by Frank Pooler in 1946
Composed by Richard Carpenter in 1970
Performed by The Carpenters in 1970

Greeting cards have all been sent
The Christmas rush is through
I still have one wish to make
A special one for you

Merry Christmas, darling
We're apart, that's true
But I can dream, and in my dreams
I'm Christmas-ing with you

Holidays are joyful
There's always something new
But every day's a holiday
When I'm near to you

Oh, the lights on my tree
I wish you could see, I wish it every day
Logs on the fire, fill me with desire
To see you and to say
That I wish you Merry Christmas
(Merry Christmas, darling)
Happy New Year, too
I've just one wish on this Christmas Eve
(On this Christmas Eve)
I wish I were with you

Logs on the fire, fill me with desire
To see you and to say
That I wish you Merry Christmas
(Merry Christmas, darling)
Happy New Year, too
I've just one wish on this Christmas Eve
(On this Christmas Eve)
I wish I were with you
I wish I were with you

Merry Merry Merry Christmas
Merry Christmas, Darling

Mistletoe and Holly

*Written and Composed by Frank Sinatra, Dok Stanford and Henry W.
Sanicola in 1957*

Oh by gosh, by golly,
It's time for mistletoe and holly,
Tasty pheasants, Christmas presents,
Country sides covered with snow.
Oh by gosh, by jingle,
It's time for carols and Kris Kringle.

Over-eating, merry greeting
From relatives you don't know.
Then comes that big night,
Giving the tree the trim.
You'll hear voices by starlight,
Singing a Yuletide hymn.

Oh by gosh, by golly,
It's time for mistletoe and holly,
Fancy ties and Granny's pies
And folks stealing a kiss or two,
As they whisper Merry Christmas to you.

Then comes that big night,
Giving the tree the trim.

You'll hear voices by starlight,
Singing a Yuletide hymn.

Oh by gosh, by golly,
It's time for mistletoe and holly,
Fancy ties and Granny's pies
And folks stealing a kiss or two,
As they whisper Merry Christmas to you.

Must Be Santa

Composed by the polka band Brave Combo

Who's got a beard that's long and white?
Santa's got a beard that's long and white.

Who comes around on a special night?
Santa comes around on a special night.

Special night, beard that's white.

Must be Santa,
Must be Santa,
Must be Santa, Santa Claus.

Who wears boots and a suit of red?
Santa wears boots and a suit of red.

Who wears a long cap on his head?
Santa wears a long cap on his head.

Cap on head, suit that's red.
Special night, beard that's white.

Must be Santa,
Must be Santa,
Must be Santa, Santa Claus.

Who's got a big red cherry nose?
Santa's got a big red cherry nose.

Who laughs this way?
HO HO HO!
Santa laughs this way,
HO HO HO.

HO HO HO, cherry nose,
Cap on head, suit that's red,
Special night, beard that's white.

Must be Santa,
Must be Santa,
Must be Santa, Santa Claus.

Who very soon will come our way?
Santa very soon will come our way.

Eight little reindeer pull his sleigh,
Santa's little reindeer pull his sleigh.

Reindeer sleigh, come our way,
HO HO HO, cherry nose,
Cap on head, suit that's red,
Special night, beard that's white.

Must be Santa,
Must be Santa,
Must be Santa, Santa Claus.

Dasher, Dancer, Prancer, Vixen,
Comet, Cupid, Donner and Blitzen.

Reindeer sleigh, come our way,
HO HO HO, cherry nose,
Cap on head, suit that's red,
Special night, beard that's white.

Must be Santa,
Must be Santa,
Must be Santa, Santa Claus.

O Christmas Tree

Author Unknown
Based on Traditional German Carol

O Christmas tree! O Christmas tree!
Thy leaves are so unchanging;
O Christmas tree! O Christmas tree!
Thy leaves are so unchanging;
Not only green when summer's here,
But also when 'tis cold and drear.
O Christmas tree! O Christmas tree!
Thy leaves are so unchanging!

O Christmas tree! O Christmas tree!
Much pleasure thou can'st give me;
O Christmas tree! O Christmas tree!
Much pleasure thou can'st give me;
How often has the Christmas tree,
Afforded me the greatest glee!
O Christmas tree! O Christmas tree!
Much pleasure thou can'st give me.

O Christmas tree! O Christmas tree!
Thy candles shine so brightly!
O Christmas tree! O Christmas tree!
Thy candles shine so brightly!
From base to summit, gay and bright,
There's only splendor for the sight.
O Christmas tree! O Christmas tree!
Thy candles shine so brightly!

O Christmas tree! O Christmas tree!
How richly God has decked Thee!
O Christmas tree! O Christmas tree!
How richly God has decked Thee!
Thou bidst us true and faithful be,
And trust in God unchangingly.
O Christmas tree! O Christmas tree!
How richly God has decked Thee!

Alternative

Composed by Kathy Parson for the album "Simply Christmas"

Oh Christmas tree! Oh Christmas tree!
How steadfast are your branches!
Your boughs are green, in summer's clime,
And through the snows of wintertime.
Oh Christmas tree! Oh Christmas tree!
How steadfast are your branches!

Oh Christmas tree! Oh Christmas tree!
What happiness befalls me.
When oft at joyous Christmas-time,
Your form inspires my song and rhyme.
Oh Christmas tree! Oh Christmas tree!
What happiness befalls me.

Oh Christmas tree! Oh Christmas tree!
Your boughs can teach a lesson,
That constant faith and hope sublime,
Lend strength and comfort through all time.
Oh Christmas tree! Oh Christmas tree!
Your boughs can teach a lesson.

Alternative 2

Written by Ernst Anschute in 1824 (German Origin)

O Christmas tree, O Christmas tree!
How are Thy leaves so verdant!
O Christmas tree, O Christmas tree!
How are Thy leaves so verdant!

Not only in the summertime,
But even in winter is Thy prime.
O Christmas tree, O Christmas tree,
How are Thy leaves so verdant!

O Christmas tree, O Christmas tree,
Much pleasure doth thou bring me!
O Christmas tree, O Christmas tree,
Much pleasure doth thou bring me!

For every year the Christmas tree,
Brings to us all both joy and glee.
O Christmas tree, O Christmas tree,
Much pleasure doth thou bring me!

O Christmas tree, O Christmas tree,
Thy candles shine out brightly!
O Christmas tree, O Christmas tree,
Thy candles shine out brightly!

Each bough doth hold its tiny light,
That makes each toy to sparkle bright.
O Christmas tree, O Christmas tree,
Thy candles shine out brightly!

O Come All Ye Faithful

Based on a traditional Latin hymn "Adeste Fidelis" which is attributed to John Wade
Composed by John Reading in the early 1700s

O come, all ye faithful
Joyful and triumphant,
O come ye, O come ye to Bethlehem.
Come and behold Him,
Born the King of angels.

O come, let us adore Him,
O come, let us adore Him,
O come, let us adore Him,
Christ the Lord.

Sing, choirs of angels,
Sing in exultation.
O sing, all ye citizens of Heaven above,
Glory to God in the highest.

O come, let us adore Him,
O come, let us adore Him,
O come, let us adore Him,
Christ the Lord.

All Hail! Lord, we greet Thee,
Born this happy morning;
O Jesus! For evermore be Thy name adored.
Word of the Father,
Now in flesh appearing.

O come, let us adore Him,
O come, let us adore Him,
O come, let us adore Him,
Christ the Lord.

O Holy Night

Based on a French carol "Minuit, Chretiens"
Written by Placide Cappeau de Roquemaure in 1847
Music composed by Adolphe Adam
Translated to English by John Sullivan Dwight

O holy night! The stars are brightly shining,
It is the night of the dear Saviour's birth.
Long lay the world in sin and error pining.
Till He appeared and the Spirit felt its worth.
A thrill of hope the weary world rejoices,
For yonder breaks a new and glorious morn.
Fall on your knees! Oh, hear the angel voices!
O night divine, the night when Christ was born;
O night, O holy night, O night divine!
O night, O holy night, O night divine!

Led by the light of faith serenely beaming,
With glowing hearts by His cradle we stand.
O'er the world a star is sweetly gleaming,
Now come the Wiseman from out of the Orient land.
The King of kings lay thus lowly manger;
In all our trials born to be our friends.
He knows our need, our weakness is no stranger,
Behold your King! Before him lowly bend!
Behold your King! Before him lowly bend!

Truly He taught us to love one another,
His law is love and His gospel is peace.
Chains he shall break, for the slave is our brother.
And in his name all oppression shall cease.
Sweet hymns of joy in grateful chorus raise we,
With all our hearts we praise His holy name.
Christ is the Lord! Then ever, ever praise we,
His power and glory ever more proclaim!
His power and glory ever more proclaim!

O Little Town of Bethlehem

Written by Bishop Phillips Brooks in 1868
Music by Lewis Henry Redner

O little town of Bethlehem,
How still we see Thee lie!
Above Thy deep and dreamless sleep
The silent stars go by.
Yet in Thy dark streets shineth
The everlasting Light;
The hopes and fears of all the years
Are met in Thee tonight.

O morning stars, together
Proclaim the holy birth!
And praises sing to God the King,
And peace to men on earth.
For Christ is born of Mary
And gathered all above,
While mortals sleep the Angels keep
Their watch of wondering love.

How silently, how silently,
The wondrous gift is given;
So God imparts to human hearts
The blessings of His Heaven.
No ear may hear His coming,
But in this world of sin,
Where meek souls will receive Him still,
The dear Christ enters in.

Where children pure and happy
Pray to the blessed Child,
Where misery cries out to Thee,
Son of the Mother mild;
Where charity stands watching
And faith holds wide the door,
The dark night wakes, the glory breaks,
And Christmas comes once more.

O holy Child of Bethlehem
Descend to us, we pray!
Cast our sin and enter in,
Be born to us today.
We hear the Christmas angels,
The great glad tidings tell;
O come to us, abide with us,
Our Lord Emmanuel!

Alternative (2nd Verse)

For Christ is born of Mary,
And gathered all above,
While mortals sleep, the angels keep
Their watch of wondering love.
O morning stars, together,
Proclaim the holy birth,
And praises sing to God the King,
And peace to men on earth!

Please Come Home for Christmas
(Bells Will Be Ringing)

Written by Charles Brown and Gene Redd in 1960

Bells will be ringing, the glad, glad news;
Oh, what a Christmas, to have the blues;
My baby's gone;
I have no friends;
To wish me greetings, once again;
Choirs will be singing, "Silent Night";
Oh, Christmas carols, by candlelight.

Please come home for Christmas;
Please come home for Christmas;
If not for Christmas, by New Year's night.

Friends and relations,
Send salutations,
Just as sure as the stars shine above.

This is Christmas, Christmas my dear,
The time of year to be with the one that you love.

Then will you tell me, you'll never more roam,
Christmas and New Year will find you home.
There'll be no more sorrow,
No grief or pain,
'Cause I'll be happy that it's Christmas once again.

Rockin' Around the Christmas Tree

Composed by Johnny Marks
Performed by Brenda Lee in 1958

Rockin' around the Christmas tree,
At the Christmas party hop.
Mistletoe hung where you can see,
Every couple tries to stop.

Rockin' around the Christmas tree,
Let the Christmas spirit ring.
Later we'll have some pumpkin pie,
And we'll do some caroling.

You will get a sentimental
Feeling when you hear,
Voices singing "Let's be jolly,
Deck the halls with boughs of holly."

Rockin' around the Christmas tree,
Have a happy holiday.
Everyone dancing merrily,
In the new old-fashioned way.

Rudolph, the Red Nosed Reindeer

Written by Robert L May in 1939
Music by Johnny Marks
Performed by Gene Autry in 1949

You know Dasher and Dancer
And Prancer and Vixen
Comet and Cupid
And Donner and Blitzen.
But do you recall
The most famous reindeer of all?

Rudolph, the red-nosed reindeer
Had a very shiny nose
And if you ever saw it
You would even say it glows

All of the other reindeer
Used to laugh and call him names
They never let poor Rudolph
Join in any reindeer games

Then one foggy Christmas Eve
Santa came to say
"Rudolph with your nose so bright
Won't you guide my sleigh tonight?"

Then all the reindeer loved him
And they shouted out with glee
"Rudolph, the red-nosed reindeer
You'll go down in history!"

Santa Baby

Written by Joan Javits, Philip Springer, and Tony Springer
Performed by Eartha Kitt in 1953

Santa baby,
Slip a sable under the tree for me.
Been an awful good girl,
Santa baby,
So hurry down the chimney tonight.

Santa baby,
A '54 convertible too,
Light blue.
I'll wait up for you, dear,
Santa baby,
So hurry down the chimney tonight.

Think of all the fun I've missed,
Think of all the fellas,
I haven't kissed.
Next year I could be just as good,
If you'll check off my Christmas list.

Santa baby,
I want a yacht,
And really, that's not a lot,
Been an angel all year,
Santa baby,
So hurry down the chimney tonight.

Santa honey,
One little thing
I really need the deed
To a platinum mine,
Santa honey,
So hurry down the chimney tonight.

Santa cutie,
And fill my stocking
With a duplex and checks.
Sign your 'X' on the line,

Santa cutie,
And hurry down the chimney tonight.

Come and trim my Christmas tree,
With some decorations
Bought at Tiffany's,
I really do believe in you,
Let's see if you believe in me.

Santa baby,
Forgot to mention one little thing,
A ring.
I don't mean on the phone,
Santa baby,
So hurry down the chimney tonight.

Hurry down the chimney tonight,
Hurry, tonight.

Santa Claus is Coming to Town

Written by Haven Gillespie in 1932
Composed by John Fredrick Coots in 1934

You better watch out,
You better not cry,
You better not pout,
I'm telling you why:
Santa Claus is coming to town.

He's making a list,
And checking it twice;
Gonna find out
Who's naughty or nice.
Santa Claus is coming to town.

He sees you when you're sleeping.
He knows when you're awake.
He knows if you've been bad or good,
So be good for goodness sake!

Oh, you better watch out!
You better not cry.
Better not pout,
I'm telling you why:
Santa Claus is coming to town.
Santa Claus is coming to town!

Silent Night

Written by Joseph Mohr (in German)
Music by Franz Gruber
Translated to English by John Young

Silent night, holy night,
All is calm, all is bright.
Round yon Virgin, Mother and Child,
Holy Infant, so tender and mild.
Sleep in heavenly peace,
Sleep in heavenly peace.

Silent night, holy night,
Shepherds quake at the sight.
Glories stream from Heaven afar,
Heavenly hosts sing Alleluia!
Christ the Saviour is born,
Christ the Saviour is born!

Silent night, holy night,
Son of God, love's pure light.
Radiant beams from Thy holy face,
With dawn of redeeming grace.
Jesus, Lord, at Thy birth,
Jesus, Lord, at Thy birth.

Silent night, holy night,
Wondrous star lend Thy light.
With the angels let us sing,
Alleluia to our King.
Christ the Saviour is here,
Christ the Saviour is here!

Silver and Gold

Written By Johnny Marks
Performed by Burt Ives
From the animated movie "Rudolph, The Red Nosed Reindeer"

Silver and gold,
Silver and gold.
Everyone wishes for silver and gold,
How do you measure it's worth?
Just by the pleasure it gives here on earth.

Silver and gold,
Silver and gold.
Mean so much more when I see
Silver and gold decorations,
On every Christmas tree.

{Spoken}
What's a Christmas tree without tinsel,
And pretty silver and gold decorations?
Can't really call it a Christmas tree now can you?

And think of all the fun and joy
That would be lost on Christmas morning
If all the young folks didn't get to see
That sparkling happy tree.

Silver and gold,
Silver and gold.
Mean so much more when I see
Silver and gold decorations
On every Christmas tree.

Silver Bells

Written by Jay Livingston and Ray Evans in 1951
Performed by Bob Hope and Marilyn Maxwell
Later Performed by Bing Crosby and Carol Richards

Silver bells, silver bells,
It's Christmas time in the city.
Ring-a-ling, hear them ring,
Soon it will be Christmas day.

City sidewalks, busy sidewalks,
Dressed in holiday style.
In the air there's a feeling of Christmas,
Children laughing, people passing,
Meeting smile after smile.
And on every street corner you'll hear

Silver bells, silver bells,
It's Christmas time in the city.
Ring-a-ling, hear them ring,
Soon it will be Christmas day.

Strings of street lights, even stop lights,
Blink a bright red and green.
As the shoppers rush home with their treasures.
Hear the snow crunch, see the kids bunch,
This is Santa's big day,
And above all this bustle you'll hear.

Silver bells, silver bells,
It's Christmas time in the city.
Ring-a-ling, hear them sing,
Soon it will be Christmas day.
Soon it will be Christmas day.

Sleigh Ride

Written by Mitchell Parish
Music by Leroy Anderson in 1948

Just hear those sleigh bells jingle-ing
Ring ting tingle-ing too
Come on, it's lovely weather
For a sleigh ride together with you

Outside the snow is falling
And friends are calling "You Hoo"
Come on, it's lovely weather
For a sleigh ride together with you

Giddy-yup giddy-yup giddy-yup
Let's go, let's look at the show
We're riding in a wonderland of snow
Giddy-yup giddy-yup giddy-yup
It's grand, just holding your hand
We're gliding along with a song
Of a wintry fairy land

Our cheeks are nice and rosy
And comfy cozy are we
We're snuggled up together
Like two birds of a feather would be
Let's take the road before us
And sing a chorus or two
Come on, it's lovely weather
For a sleigh ride together with you

There's a birthday party
At the home of Farmer Gray
It'll be the perfect ending for a perfect day
We'll be singing the songs
We love to sing without a single stop
At the fireplace while we watch
The chestnuts pop
Pop! Pop! Pop!

There's a happy feeling
Nothing in the world can buy
When they pass around the chocolate
And the pumpkin pie
It'll nearly be like a picture print
By Currier and Ives
These wonderful things are the things
We remember all through our lives

Just hear those sleigh bells jingle-ing
Ring ting tingle-ing too
Come on, it's lovely weather
For a sleigh ride together with you

Outside the snow is falling
And friends are calling "You Hoo"
Come on, it's lovely weather
For a sleigh ride together with you

Giddy-yup giddy-yup giddy-yup
Let's go, let's look at the show
We're riding in a wonderland of snow
Giddy-yup giddy-yup giddy-yup
It's grand, just holding your hand
We're gliding along with a song
Of a wintry fairy land

Our cheeks are nice and rosy
And comfy cozy are we
We're snuggled up together
Like two birds of a feather would be
Let's take the road before us
And sing a chorus or two
Come on, it's lovely weather
For a sleigh ride together with you

That Christmas Feeling

Written by Bennie Benjamin
Composed by George Weiss
Performed by Perry Como
in 1946

When the days of December are numbered
And the earth begs it's snowflakes to fall
That's the time of the year that Christmas is here
With peace and goodwill for all

How I love that Christmas feelin'
How I treasure it's friendly glow
See the way a stranger greets you
Just as though you'd met him Christmases ago

Christmas helps you to remember
To do what other folks hold dear
What a blessed place the world would be
If we had that Christmas feelin' all year

Christmas helps you to remember
To do what other folks hold dear
What a blessed place the world would be
If we had that Christmas feelin' all year

The Christmas Song
(Chestnuts Roasting on an Open Fire)

Written by Mel Torme and R. Wells
Performed by Nat King Cole.

Chestnuts roasting on an open fire,
Jack Frost nipping at your nose.
Yuletide carols being sung by a choir,
And folks dressed up like Eskimos.

Everybody knows, a turkey and some mistletoe,
Help to make the season bright.
Tiny tots with their eyes all aglow,
Will find it hard to sleep tonight.

They know that Santa's on his way,
He's loaded lots of toys and goodies on his sleigh.
And every mother's child is gonna spy,
To see if reindeer really know how to fly.

And so I'm offering this simple phrase,
To kids from one to ninety-two.
Although it's been said many times, many ways,
"Merry Christmas to you."

And so I'm offering this simple phrase,
To kids from one to ninety-two.
Although it's been said many times, many ways,
"Merry Christmas to you."

The First Noel

Author Unknown
Traditional English Carol
Written in the Sixteenth Century

The First Noel, the angels did say,
Was to certain poor shepherds in fields as they lay,
In fields where they lay keeping their sheep,
On a cold winter's night that was so deep.

Noel, Noel, Noel, Noel.
Born is the King of Israel!

They looked up and saw a star,
Shining in the East beyond them far,
And to the earth it gave great light,
And so it continued both day and night.

Noel, Noel, Noel, Noel.
Born is the King of Israel!

And by the light of that same star,
Three Wise men came from country far,
To seek for a King was their intent,
And to follow the star wherever it went.

Noel, Noel, Noel, Noel.
Born is the King of Israel!

This star drew nigh to the northwest,
O'er Bethlehem it took its rest,
And there it did both pause and stay,
Right o'er the place where Jesus lay.

Noel, Noel, Noel, Noel.
Born is the King of Israel!

Then entered in those wise men three,
Full reverently upon their knee,
And offered there in His presence,
Their gold and myrrh and frankincense.

Noel, Noel, Noel, Noel.
Born is the King of Israel!

Then let us all with one accord,
Sing praises to our heavenly Lord,
That hath made Heaven and Earth of nought,
And with his blood mankind has bought.

Noel, Noel, Noel, Noel.
Born is the King of Israel!

If we in our time shall do well,
We shall be free from death and hell.
For God hath prepared for us all,
A resting place in general.

Noel, Noel, Noel, Noel.
Born is the King of Israel!

The Night Before Christmas

T'was the night before Christmas, when all through the
house,
Not a creature was stirring, not even a mouse.
The stockings were hung, by the chimney with care,
In hopes that St. Nicholas, soon would be there.

The children were nestled all snug in their beds,
While visions of sugar-plums danced in their heads.
And mamma in her 'kerchief, and I in my cap,
Had just settled our brains for a long winter's nap.

When out on the lawn there arose such a clatter,
I sprang from the bed to see what was the matter.
Away to the window I flew like a flash,
Tore open the shutters and threw up the sash.

The moon on the breast of the new-fallen snow
Gave the lustre of mid-day to objects below.
When, what to my wondering eyes should appear,
But a miniature sleigh, and eight tiny reindeer.

With a little old driver, so lively and quick,
I knew in a moment it must be St. Nick.
More rapid than eagles his coursers they came,
And he whistled, and shouted, and called them by name!

"Now Dasher! Now, Dancer! Now, Prancer and Vixen!
On, Comet! On, Cupid! On, Donner and Blitzen!
To the top of the porch! To the top of the wall!
Now dash away! Dash away! Dash away all!"

As dry leaves that before the wild hurricane fly,
When they meet with an obstacle, mount to the sky.
So up to the house-top the coursers they flew,
With the sleigh full of toys, and St. Nicholas too.

And then, in a twinkling, I heard on the roof
The prancing and pawing of each little hoof.
As I drew in my head, and was turning around,
Down the chimney St. Nicholas came with a bound.

He was dressed all in fur, from his head to his foot,
And his clothes were all tarnished with ashes and soot.
A bundle of toys he had flung on his back,
And he looked like a peddler, just opening his pack.

His eyes, how they twinkled! His dimples, how merry!
His cheeks were like roses, his nose like a cherry!
His droll little mouth was drawn up like a bow,
And the beard of his chin was as white as the snow.

The stump of a pipe he held tight in his teeth,
And the smoke it encircled his head like a wreath.
He had a broad face and a little round belly,
That shook when he laughed, like a bowlful of jelly!

He was chubby and plump, a right jolly old elf,
And I laughed when I saw him, in spite of myself!
A wink of his eye and a twist of his head,
Soon gave me to know I had nothing to dread.

He spoke not a word, but went straight to his work,
And filled all the stockings, then turned with a jerk.
And laying his finger aside of his nose,
And giving a nod, up the chimney he rose!

He sprang to his sleigh, to his team gave a whistle,
And away they all flew like the down of a thistle.
But I heard him exclaim, 'ere he drove out of sight,
"Happy Christmas to all, and to all a good-night!"

85

The Twelve Days of Christmas

Traditional Christmas Song based on a French Carol
The twelve days between the birthday of Jesus (Dec 25) and the day of
the Epiphany, when the baby Jesus was visited by the wise men (Jan 6).

On the first day of Christmas,
My true love sent to me
A partridge in a pear tree.

On the second day of Christmas,
My true love sent to me
Two turtle doves,
And a partridge in a pear tree.

On the third day of Christmas,
My true love sent to me
Three French hens,
Two turtle doves,
And a partridge in a pear tree.

On the fourth day of Christmas,
My true love sent to me
Four calling birds,
Three French hens,
Two turtle doves,
And a partridge in a pear tree.

On the fifth day of Christmas,
My true love sent to me
Five golden rings,
Four calling birds,
Three French hens,
Two turtle doves,
And a partridge in a pear tree.

On the sixth day of Christmas,
My true love sent to me
Six geese a-laying,
Five golden rings,
Four calling birds,
Three French hens,

Two turtle doves,
And a partridge in a pear tree.

On the seventh day of Christmas,
My true love sent to me
Seven swans a-swimming,
Six geese a-laying,
Five golden rings,
Four calling birds,
Three French hens,
Two turtle doves,
And a partridge in a pear tree.

On the eighth day of Christmas,
My true love sent to me
Eight maids a-milking,
Seven swans a-swimming,
Six geese a-laying,
Five golden rings,
Four calling birds,
Three French hens,
Two turtle doves,
And a partridge in a pear tree.

On the ninth day of Christmas,
My true love sent to me
Nine ladies dancing,
Eight maids a-milking,
Seven swans a-swimming,
Six geese a-laying,
Five golden rings,
Four calling birds,
Three French hens,
Two turtle doves,
And a partridge in a pear tree.

On the tenth day of Christmas,
My true love sent to me
Ten lords a-leaping,
Nine ladies dancing,
Eight maids a-milking,
Seven swans a-swimming,

Six geese a-laying,
Five golden rings,
Four calling birds,
Three French hens,
Two turtle doves,
And a partridge in a pear tree.

On the eleventh day of Christmas,
My true love sent to me
Eleven pipers piping,
Ten lords a-leaping,
Nine ladies dancing,
Eight maids a-milking,
Seven swans a-swimming,
Six geese a-laying,
Five golden rings,
Four calling birds,
Three French hens,
Two turtle doves,
And a partridge in a pear tree.

On the twelfth day of Christmas,
My true love sent to me
Twelve drummers drumming,
Eleven pipers piping,
Ten lords a-leaping,
Nine ladies dancing,
Eight maids a-milking,
Seven swans a-swimming,
Six geese a-laying,
Five golden rings,
Four calling birds,
Three French hens,
Two turtle doves,
And a partridge in a pear tree!

This Christmas

By Nadine McKinnor and Donny Hathaway

Hang all the mistletoe
I'm gonna get to know you better
This Christmas

And as we trim the tree
How much fun it's gonna be together
This Christmas

Fireside is blazing bright
We're caroling through the night
And this Christmas will be
A very special Christmas for me

Presents and cards are here
My world is filled with cheer and you
This Christmas

And as I look around
Your eyes outshine the town, they do
This Christmas

Fireside is blazing bright
We're caroling through the night
And this Christmas will be
A very special Christmas for me

Shake a hand, shake a hand now

Fireside blazing bright
We're caroling through the night
And this Christmas, will be
A very special Christmas, for me

Hang all the mistletoe
I'm gonna get to know you better
This Christmas

And as we trim the tree
How much fun it's gonna be together
This Christmas

Fireside is blazing bright
We're caroling through the night
And this Christmas will be
A very special Christmas for me

Merry Christmas
Shake a hand, shake a hand now
Wish your brother "Merry Christmas"
All over the land

Up on the Housetop

Written and Composed by Benjamin R. Hanby, circa 1860

Up on the housetop reindeer pause,
Out jumps good old Santa Claus.
Down through the chimney with lots of toys,
All for the little ones, Christmas joys.

Ho, ho, ho! Who wouldn't go!
Ho, ho, ho! Who wouldn't go!
Up on the housetop, click, click, click,
Down through the chimney with good Saint Nick.

First comes the stocking of little Nell,
Oh, dear Santa, fill it well;
Give her a dolly that laughs and cries,
One that will open and shut her eyes.

Ho, ho, ho! Who wouldn't go!
Ho, ho, ho! Who wouldn't go!
Up on the housetop, click, click, click,
Down through the chimney with good Saint Nick.

Look in the stocking of little Bill,
Oh, just see that glorious fill!
Here is a hammer and lots of tacks,
A whistle and a ball and a set of jacks.

Ho, ho, ho! Who wouldn't go!
Ho, ho, ho! Who wouldn't go!
Up on the housetop, click, click, click,
Down through the chimney with good Saint Nick.

We Three Kings of Orient Are

Written and Composed by John Henry Hopkins, Jr. in 1857

We three Kings of Orient are,
Bearing gifts we traverse afar,
Field and fountain, moor and mountain,
Following yonder star.

O, star of wonder, star of night,
Star with royal beauty bright,
Westward leading, still proceeding,
Guide us to Thy perfect light.

Born a King on Bethlehem plain,
Gold I bring to crown Him again,
King forever,
Ceasing never,
Over us all to reign.

O, star of wonder, star of night,
Star with royal beauty bright,
Westward leading, still proceeding,
Guide us to Thy perfect light.

Frankincense to offer have I,
Incense owns a Deity nigh;
Prayer and praising,
All men raising,
Worship Him, God on high.

O, star of wonder, star of night,
Star with royal beauty bright,
Westward leading, still proceeding,
Guide us to Thy perfect light.

Myrrh is mine; its bitter perfume,
Breathes a life of gathering gloom;
Sorrowing, sighing,
Bleeding, dying,
Sealed in the stone-cold tomb.

O, star of wonder, star of night,
Star with royal beauty bright,
Westward leading, still proceeding,
Guide us to Thy perfect light.

Glorious now behold Him arise,
King and God and sacrifice.
Heaven sings, "Hallelujah!"
"Hallelujah!" Earth replies.

O, star of wonder, star of night,
Star with royal beauty bright,
Westward leading, still proceeding,
Guide us to Thy perfect light.

We Wish You A Merry Christmas

Traditional English Carol
Written in the Sixteenth Century

We wish you a Merry Christmas,
We wish you a Merry Christmas,
We wish you a Merry Christmas,
And a Happy New Year!

Good tidings we bring
To you and your kin;
Good tidings for Christmas
And a Happy New Year.

Now bring us some figgy pudding,
Now bring us some figgy pudding,
Now bring us some figgy pudding,
And a cup of good cheer.

Good tidings we bring
To you and your kin;
Good tidings for Christmas
And a Happy New Year.

We all like our figgy pudding,
We all like our figgy pudding,
We all like our figgy pudding,
With all its good cheer.

Good tidings we bring
To you and your kin;
Good tidings for Christmas
And a Happy New Year.

We won't go until we get some,
We won't go until we get some,
We won't go until we get some,
So bring some out here.

Good tidings we bring
To you and your kin;

Good tidings for Christmas
And a Happy New Year.

We wish you a Merry Christmas,
We wish you a Merry Christmas,
We wish you a Merry Christmas,
And a Happy New Year!
And a Happy New Year!

Good tidings we bring
To you and your kin;
Good tidings for Christmas
And a Happy New Year.

Alternative

We wish you a Merry Christmas,
We wish you a Merry Christmas,
We wish you a Merry Christmas,
And a Happy New Year!

Good tidings to you,
And all of your kin,
Good tidings for Christmas,
And a Happy New Year.

We all know that Santa's coming,
We all know that Santa's coming,
We all know that Santa's coming,
And soon will be here.

Good tidings to you,
And all of your kin,
Good tidings for Christmas,
And a Happy New Year.

We wish you a Merry Christmas,
We wish you a Merry Christmas,
We wish you a Merry Christmas,
And a Happy New Year!

What Child is This?

Written by William Chatterton Dix in 1865
Music is a traditional 16th Century melody called Greensleeves

What child is this, who, laid to rest,
On Mary's lap is sleeping,
Whom angels greet with anthems sweet,
While shepherds watch are keeping?

This, this is Christ the King,
Whom shepherds guard and angels sing,
Haste, haste to bring Him laud,
The babe, the son of Mary!

Why lies he in such mean estate,
Where ox and ass are feeding?
Good Christians, fear, for sinners here,
The silent word is pleading.

Nails, spear shall pierce Him through,
The cross be borne for me, for you.
Hail, hail the word made flesh,
The babe, the son of Mary!

So bring him incense, gold, and myrrh,
Come, peasant, King, to own Him!
The King of kings salvation brings,
Let loving hearts enthrone Him!

Raise, raise a song on high,
The virgin sings her lullaby.
Joy, joy for Christ is born,
The babe, the son of Mary!

White Christmas

Written by Irving Berlin in 1940
Performed by Bing Crosby and other various artists

I'm dreaming of a white Christmas,
Just like the ones I used to know.
Where the treetops glisten,
And children listen,
To hear sleigh bells in the snow.

I'm dreaming of white Christmas,
With every Christmas card I write.
May your days be merry and bright,
And may all your Christmases be white.

I'm dreaming of a white Christmas,
Just like the ones I used to know.
Where the treetops glisten,
And children listen,
To hear sleigh bells in the snow.

I'm dreaming of a white Christmas,
With every Christmas card I write.
May your days be merry and bright,
And may all your Christmases be white.

Winter Wonderland

Written by Richard Smith and Composed by Felix Barnard in 1934

Sleigh bells ring, are you listening?
In the lane, snow is glistening.
It's a beautiful sight.
We're happy tonight,
Walking in a winter wonderland.

Gone away, is the bluebird.
Here to stay, is the new bird.
He sings a love song
As we go along,
Walking in a winter wonderland.

In the meadow we can build a snowman
Then pretend that he is Parson Brown.

He'll say, "Are you married?"
We'll say, "No, man,
But you can do the job
When you're in town."

Later on, we'll conspire
As we dream by the fire
To face unafraid,
The plans that we made
Walking in a winter wonderland

In the meadow we can build a snowman,
And pretend that he's a circus clown
We'll have lots of fun with mister snowman,
Until the other kids knock him down.

When it snows, ain't it thrilling,
Though your nose gets a chilling
We'll frolic and play, the Eskimo way,
Walking in a winter wonderland.

Walking in a winter wonderland,
Walking in a winter wonderland.

End Notes

Thank you for your purchase. I hope you enjoyed all the Christmas songs!

If you enjoyed this ebook, please take a moment to post a review and share with your friends. If you were unsatisfied with this ebook, please let me know using the contact details below.

Please send me your comments and suggestions. Any feedback is greatly appreciated.

Connect with the Author Online

Author.JenniferEdwards@gmail.com

http://www.smashwords.com/profile/view/jenniferedwards

Made in United States
Orlando, FL
16 December 2022